For Your Wedding

C A K E S

For Your Wedding

CAKES

Bette Matthews

FRIEDMAN/FAIRFAX
PUBLISHERS

A FRIEDMAN/FAIRFAX BOOK

© 2001 by Michael Friedman Publishing Group, Inc.

Please visit our website: www.metrobooks.com

Library of Congress Cataloging-in-Publication Data

Matthews, Bette.
   Cakes / by Bette Matthews.
      p. cm. — (For your wedding)
   Includes bibliographical references and index.
   ISBN 1-56799-961-1
    1. Wedding Cakes. 2. Cake decorating. I. Title. II. Series.

TX771 .M315 2000
641.8′653—dc21

                                             00-021286

Editor: Ann Kirby
Art Director: Jeff Batzli
Designer: Jennifer O'Connor
Photography Editors: Kate Perry and Valerie Kennedy
Production Manager: Camille Lee

Color separations by Colourscan Overseas Co Pte Ltd
Printed in China by C&C Offset Printing Co., Ltd.

3 5 7 9 10 8 6 4 2

Distributed by Sterling Publishing Co., Inc.
387 Park Avenue South
New York, NY 10016
Distributed in Canada by Sterling Publishing
Canada Manda Group
One Atlantic Avenue, Suite 105
Toronto, Ontario, Canada M6K 3E7
Distributed in Australia by
Capricorn Link (Australia) Pty, Ltd.
P.O. Box 704, Windsor, NSW 2756 Australiap

CONTENTS

INTRODUCTION

*A*ccording to Emily Post, the diva of etiquette, the only element necessary to create a wedding reception, other than the bride and groom of course, is a wedding cake. While this may seem like a huge responsibility for a simple confection, even the simplest of wedding cakes can turn a happy gathering into a grand celebration. Whether your cake is a stately mountain of snowy frosting and royal icing blossoms, or a single, porcelain-finished round layer cake adorned with one perfect rose, your wedding cake will reflect the style and essence of this joyous day.

Just as the bride stands out amidst the assemblage of all present at a wedding ceremony, the wedding cake is also the center of attention—the *pièce de résistance*—at a reception. Proudly displayed throughout the reception as a work of art, the wedding cake forms a focal point around which other elements of the reception

PAGE 6: A WEDDING CAKE
SHOULD BE DELICIOUS
AS WELL AS BEAUTIFUL.
HERE, FOUR TIERS OF
RICH RASPBERRY LAYER
CAKE ARE TOPPED WITH A
COATING OF STUNNING—AND
SCRUMPTIOUS—BUTTERCREAM.

may be built. For those who love the drama of a grand entrance, the cake can be brought in at the end of the reception, mirroring the bride's entrance during the ceremony and summoning almost as much attention. One way or another, the cake can evoke enthusiastic expectation as guests survey the mouth-watering pastry, wondering what culinary delights are in store in the first bite as they eagerly await the cake-cutting ceremony.

The multitude of choices available today are enough to make your head spin. You can indulge your cherished dreams when custom-designing your wedding cake, regardless of your spectrum of taste. There's something for everyone, whether your tastes run toward the gourmet or your grandmother's old-time recipe; toward elegance or whimsy; whether you have always dreamed of three stacked tiers of the palest pink buttercream or six layers of cappuccino cheesecake wrapped in marzipan.

The cake has had a proud history in the celebrations of societies of every era, and the wedding cake has evolved from a simple but powerful symbol of fertility into an artistic tradition with many interpretations. The people of Ancient Greece dipped a honey-laden cake in wine as part of their special feasts, and the conquering Romans adapted their own rituals to suit the occasion. For these ancient peoples, wheat was a symbol of fertility and bountiful harvest…the essence of life itself. Early records tell of guests in Ancient Rome pitching grains of wheat at the bride and groom, to encourage fertility in their union. As the custom evolved, bringing small wheat cakes to the wedding banquet became common practice. The guests would crumble the cakes over the head of the bride, evoking the same

WHO KNOWS WHAT TASTY
TREATS AWAIT WITHIN
THIS LOVELY FOUR-TIERED
MASTERPIECE? A CLASSIC
WHITE FROSTING MAY
CONCEAL DELECTABLY
DIFFERENT FLAVORS FOR
CAKE AND FILLING WITHIN
EACH TIER.

symbolic gifts of fertility and fortune. The guests would then eat the fallen crumbs to share in the young couple's good fortune. Essential for survival, wheat was considered a gift of nature, and the wedding cakes, offered as a blessing to the new union, were the perfect gift. The importance of duplicating nature's generosity was not to be underestimated in this rite, for the luck lay in the act of giving—from guest to newlyweds—and the bride who baked her own wedding wheat cakes was opening up a Pandora's box of misfortune.

By the Middle Ages, sweet buns or rolls had replaced the wheat cakes, but it was still customary for the guests to bring these treats to the wedding. Stacked into a lofty mound between the bride and groom in a towering pyramid, the buns formed a playful barrier between the newlyweds. If they were able to kiss over the stack, they would be blessed with many children and much prosperity throughout their lives.

It is said that during the seventeenth century, a French pastry chef added his signature to the custom by frosting the pyramid of cakes with sugar—thereby "gluing" the buns together and helping them retain their form. This is considered the first account of a tiered and frosted wedding confection, and from these humble beginnings, the blueprint for the modern wedding cake was born. This ancestral sweet has survived the changing times and, even today, the *croquembouche*—a tall pyramid of profiteroles, or cream puffs—is a traditional treat found at French weddings.

Until the eighteenth century, when refined flour and processed sugar became available, wedding cakes were usually dense fruitcakes baked in advance of the celebration and soaked in spirits to preserve them. The top tier would be saved for

OPPOSITE: LOOKING FOR SOMETHING A LITTLE DIFFERENT? TRY A TOWERING *CROQUEMBOUCHE*, THE TRADITIONAL FRENCH WEDDING PASTRY. CONSISTING OF A MOUNTAIN OF DELICIOUS PROFITEROLES (AND SOMETIMES HELD TOGETHER BY A LIGHT COATING OF CHOCOLATE OR CARAMEL), EACH BITE-SIZED TREAT REVEALS A DELICIOUS BURST OF RICH PASTRY CREAM.

RIGHT: A BEADED GLASS,
FOOTED CAKE STAND ADDS
HEIGHT TO THIS TOP TIER OF
A CHARMING CAKE WHILE
IT STAYS ON DISPLAY UNTIL
THE WEDDING IS OVER. THE
CATERER WILL PREPARE THE
TIER FOR YOU TO TAKE HOME
AND FREEZE FOR YOUR FIRST
ANNIVERSARY.

OPPOSITE: EVERY CAKE LOOKS
BETTER IN THE PERFECT
SETTING. WITH PRECISE
ARRANGEMENT, THE TABLE-
CLOTH CAN BE GATHERED
AND FOLDED TO CREATE
ENOUGH SURFACE INTEREST
THAT NO OTHER DECORATION
IS REQUIRED. THE SUBTLE
PATTERN AND COLOR OF
THE CLOTH DOESN'T DETRACT
FROM THE EQUALLY SUBTLE
CAKE, AND THE GOLD RIM
OF THE SCALLOPED CAKE
PLATTER IS REPEATED ON
THE CHAMPAGNE GLASSES.

the couple's first anniversary (a charming tradition that many still follow) or the

christening of their first child. This prized treat was handled with care, however,

for superstition held that if the tier crumbled before the first anniversary, the

marriage was headed for trouble.

Many of today's wedding traditions came to us from Victorian England. The Victorians' love of ornament produced elaborate, edible decorations that are still associated with a traditional wedding cake. Queen Victoria, who popularized the convention of wearing bridal white, had a cake that is said to have weighed 300 pounds (136.2kg). As confectioners grew more skillful, cakes became even more spectacular. England's Princess Elizabeth and Prince Phillip, married in 1947, had a cake that weighed in at 500 pounds (227kg) and was nine feet (2.7m) tall! Bakers began to produce architectural masterpieces. The cake at the wedding of Eunice Kennedy to Robert Sargent Shriver Jr. was eight tiers tall. Separated by columns bedecked with bows, it towered over the couple on its majestic stand. Thirty-three years later, their daughter Maria had the cake duplicated for her wedding to Arnold Schwarzenegger…columns, bows, swags, and all!

Such grand monuments are no longer the sole privilege of the rich and famous. Today's wedding cake specialists take cakes to towering heights, both literally and figuratively. Gone are the days when your choice was limited to a white cake with white frosting. Although white cake will always remain a traditional and popular option, today's bride and groom are bound only by their imaginations when selecting the elements for their cake. These days, the creation of a wedding cake has become a specialized culinary art, with many specialists setting the pace for the most sought-after cake designs and deliciously creative flavors. The baker may find inspiration in a piece of antique crystal, a gazebo in the local botanical gardens, the fabric of the bride's dress, or the theme of the event itself. Designers use color, texture, and ornament as the building blocks for the wedding cake, and

(continued on page 19)

SUGAR FLOWERS AND
VELVETY-SMOOTH EDIBLE
RIBBONS PUNCTUATE EACH
LAYER OF THIS STUNNING
WEDDING CAKE FROM
MASTER BAKER GAIL WATSON.
TINY SILVER CANDY BEADS,
OR DRAGÉES, HIGHLIGHT
THE FROSTING.

OPPOSITE: A CANDY CORNUCOPIA IS THE PERFECT CAKE TOPPER FOR THIS AUTUMNAL FRUIT BASKET. TUMBLING FROM THE TOP TIER, AN ABUNDANT HARVEST OF MARZIPAN FRUITS AND GILDED NUTS AND PINE CONES SETS THE SEASONAL MOOD. THE HARVEST-TIME THEME IS REPEATED IN THE PIPED WHEAT STALKS ADORNING THE CAKE'S SIDES, AND FINISHED OFF BY DRESSING THE TABLE IN LUXE METALLIC CLOTH SPRINKLED WITH A FEW FALLEN LEAVES.

LEFT: ENVELOPED IN SILKEN WHITE CHOCOLATE, THIS CHEERY TREAT FROM CECILE GADY OF CAKEWORK IN SAN FRANCISCO HERALDS THE SPRING SEASON WITH A RIOTOUS BURST OF GARDEN BLOSSOMS. EACH OF THE WHITE CHOCOLATE FLOWERS, MOLDED BY HAND WITH THE UTMOST ATTENTION TO DETAIL, SEEMS TO SPROUT FROM THE VERY CORE OF THIS CAKE.

new flavor combinations are introduced regularly. If you are open to anything and everything, your baker will find a combination that will tantalize your taste buds and dazzle your guests.

Whether your cake will be a gift from a talented baker in the family, your favorite local bakery, or a pastry chef who specializes in wedding cakes, don't leave choosing it until the last minute. Although some bakers require very little notice, others may get booked up months ahead, so if your requirements are very specific, start early. Have an idea of what the overall style of the wedding will be so that the cake can be tied in with the rest of the reception. Having some ideas about what you love is also helpful, as well as what you do not want under any circumstances. Visit two or three bakers to get a well-rounded view, ask to see photographs of their work, and (the best part) insist on sampling their cakes. If there's a favorite family recipe that you wish to use, discuss that with your baker. Some pastry chefs are happy to experiment…others will only use their own well-tested recipes. If you are asking the baker to try a new flavor, discuss your options for taste samples of the cake before making a final decision, and be prepared for an extra charge.

Nestled in the pages of this book are dozens upon dozens of mouth-watering treats, as pleasing to the eye as they are to the palette. Use them for inspiration, as a starting point from which you will develop the personal character of your own cake, or as a diagram for your baker to follow. Above all, enjoy the process of choosing your wedding cake. With all of the magnificent choices you have before you, the most difficult decision will be picking just one!

OPPOSITE: OFTEN THE WEDDING CAKE IS NOT THE ONLY DESSERT SERVED AT THE END OF THE RECEPTION. MANY COUPLES WISH TO OFFER THEIR GUESTS ADDITIONAL TREATS THAT COMPLEMENT THEIR CAKE IN BOTH STYLE AND FLAVOR. HERE, CLOUDS OF MERINGUE FORM AN EDIBLE BOWL FILLED WITH WHIPPED CREAM AND BERRIES, A PERFECT ACCOMPANIMENT FOR THE FLUFFY WHITE CAKE.

TOPPING
THE CAKE

PAGE 20: BURSTING WITH FLOWERS AND ORNATE DECORATIONS, THIS WELL-APPOINTED WEDDING CAKE IS GLORIOUSLY OPULENT. ITS RENAISSANCE THEME IS CONVEYED BY ITS STATELY HEIGHT, GOLD-LEAFED CHERUBS AND ORNAMENT, COFFEE-COLORED SCROLL WORK, AND LUXURIOUSLY COLORED FLOWERS, WHICH ARE ALL HANDMADE AND EDIBLE.

OPPOSITE: THE SIMPLE ADORNMENTS OF WHITE CHOCOLATE ROSES AND ROYAL ICING ROPES CREATE AN UNDERSTATED CHIC FOR THIS STYLISH DESSERT.

LEFT: SMART AND SIMPLE, THE PORCELAIN SMOOTHNESS OF FONDANT COVERING THIS CAKE IS ADORNED WITH A THIN RIBBON BORDER AT THE BASE OF EACH LAYER. ICING FLOWERS, FRUIT, AND FOLIAGE ARE PERCHED ON THE STEPS AND AROUND THE BASE OF EACH LAYER.

*T*here have never been more options for designing your wedding cake than there are today. Selecting the flavors of cake and filling is only the beginning. You must choose the frosting that will cover and enhance your cake, the types of ornaments you wish to use to embellish its design, and the crowning glory…the cake topper. Here is a brief explanation of the most common icings to help you decide which are right for you.

RIGHT: A CLOSE-UP OF THE
BAKER'S FINE CRAFTMANSHIP
SHOWS THE ATTENTION TO
DETAIL THAT RON BEN ISRAEL
PUTS INTO EACH ONE OF
HIS CAKES.

OPPOSITE: THIS ODE TO
SPRING IS BURSTING WITH
FINELY CRAFTED FLOWERS
AND FOLIAGE. AND WHAT
WOULD A GARDEN BE
WITHOUT A FLUTTERING OF
BUTTERFLIES HOVERING ABOVE
THE BOUNTIFUL BOUQUET
OF FLOWERS?

Buttercream: This rich whipped frosting is made of butter, eggs, and sugar. It can be flavored and used as filling, frosting, or for piping decorations such as flowers. Keep the cake cool; buttercream will melt in a warm room.

Fondant: Rolled fondant is a sugar dough that is rolled out onto a thin sheet, then smoothed over a cake. Its elegant matte finish looks like porcelain and

NOTHING IS MORE ROMANTIC THAN THE HEART. HERE, HEART-SHAPED CAKES ARE STACKED ONE ON TOP OF THE OTHER AND DECORATED WITH A COMBINATION OF REAL GREENERY, RIBBONS, AND SUGAR FLOWERS. THE DELICATE FREEFORM PIPING ON EACH LAYER PROVIDES A PATTERNED TEXTURE.

provides an ideal surface for decorating, but its dense, chewy texture and somewhat bland flavor do not appeal to everyone. Poured fondant is a thick sugar syrup that is poured over a cake and stiffens to a glossy finish, like that on petits fours.

Ganache: Smooth as silk, this combination of melted chocolate and cream can be whipped to a consistency suitable for filling or frosting a cake, or poured over a cake in its liquid form like poured fondant.

Royal icing: Made of sugar and egg whites, this frosting dries rock-hard upon contact with air. It is ideal for piping delicate scrolls, flowers, and borders.

BASKETWEAVE FROSTING
AND SHELL BORDERS CREATE
A LUSCIOUS BUTTERCREAM
BASE: THE PERFECT FOIL FOR
A SINGLE DRAMATIC BLOSSOM.

Marzipan: A doughy almond and sugar paste, marzipan can be molded into flowers or fruits for decoration, or rolled into sheets and draped over the cake like rolled fondant.

Whipped cream: Real heavy cream whipped to stiff peaks is wonderful for fillings, but very delicate for frostings. It does not lend itself well to piped decorations and must be kept refrigerated.

(continued on page 31)

OPPOSITE: THIS STUNNING CAKE IS FOR THE COUPLE WHO ARE NOT SHY ABOUT MAKING A STATEMENT. GOLDEN FONDANT COVERS THE BEAUTIFULLY ROUNDED SHAPES OF THE LAYERS AND BOLD FROSTING BEADS CIRCLE THE SIDES, CREATING A FABULOUS FRAME FOR THE NUTS AND LEAVES TRIMMING THE TIERS.

LEFT: GUM-PASTE ELEMENTS FLOW FROM TIER TO TIER WITH EXUBERANT EFFECT. THE MUTED TONES OF THESE DECORATIONS LEND A HINT OF AUTUMN TO THIS CAKE'S FIVE SMOOTHLY-FINISHED TIERS.

THE HEIRLOOM QUALITY OF
THIS CAKE IS UNMISTAKABLE.
DELICATE, LACY PIPING ADORNS
THE SIDES OF EACH LAYER OF
THIS FOUR-TIERED BEAUTY.
NESTLED COZILY AMIDST
THE PASTILLAGE FLOWERS
BETWEEN THE TOP TWO TIERS
IS A CHARMING MINIATURE
BRIDE AND GROOM.

Gum paste or pastillage: A dough-like substance that is edible but not very tasty, gum paste is malleable enough to form delicate flowers, ribbons, and figures. The dough becomes bone-dry when exposed to air.

Pulled or blown sugar: This complicated technique requires great skill to master. Taffy-like sugar is formed into shapes by pulling it into ribbons and molding the flat pieces, or blowing it into shapes using an air pump. It dries to a hard, glassy shine and is quite beautiful.

RIGHT: PERFECT FOR A SUMMER'S DAY, THIS PERKY PASTRY IS FROSTED WITH SMOOTH BUTTERCREAM AND EMBELLISHED WITH PIPED PEARLS OF FROSTING AND SCALLOPED SHELLS. THE BEAUTIFUL FLOWERS ADD JUST THE SMALLEST HINT OF GREEN.

OPPOSITE: SIMPLE TIERS LOOK STUNNING WHEN PAIRED WITH GENEROUS LAYERS OF FRESH FLOWERS. HERE, A PRIM DOTTED SWISS PATTERN COMPLEMENTS MOUNDS OF LUSH HYDRANGEA BLOOMS.

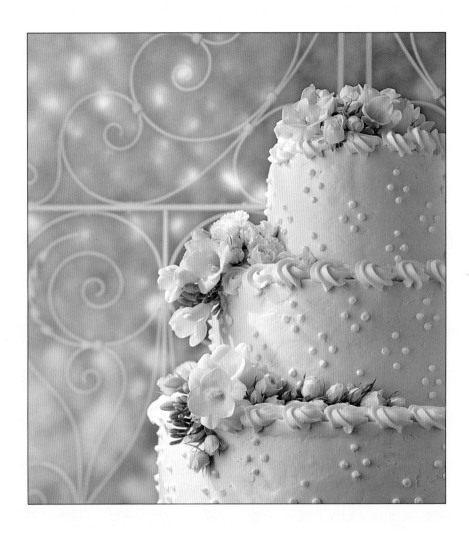

Spun sugar or angel hair: A cut whisk, dipped into melted, caramelized sugar, is waved over a suspended surface to form thin strands. The result looks like a mass of golden threads when dry, but is very delicate and will decompose in humid weather, so it must be used shortly after it is made.

(continued on page 37)

OPPOSITE: THE SQUARE SHAPE OF THE STACKED TIERS ADDS INTEREST TO THIS WEDDING CAKE. A DELICATE BUNCH OF TINY FLOWERS CONTRASTS WITH THE WIDE RIBBON CASCADING THROUGH THE BOUQUET TOPPER AND DOWN THE SIDES OF ALL THREE TIERS. NOTE HOW THE PIPING BORDERING THE TOP OF EACH TIER MIRRORS THE SCROLLS ON THE MAGNIFICENT SILVER BASE.

LEFT: HERE, A SIMILAR CAKE TOPPER RECEIVES A TOTALLY DIFFERENT TREATMENT. THIS DAISY-THEMED CAKE BY ANA PAZ IS A STUDY IN SIMPLE ELEGANCE. THE DOTTED SWISS EFFECT CREATED ON THE SIDES OF THE TOP AND BOTTOM TIER SANDWICHES THE SUBTLE DAISY PATTERNING ON THE SIDE OF THE MIDDLE TIER, REPEATED IN SUGAR FLOWERS IN THE BOUQUET AT THE TOP. SUGAR RIBBONS DRAPE ALONG THE TIERS, AND THE SLIGHTEST HINT OF YELLOW SMILES FROM EACH DAISY'S CENTER.

RIGHT: SIMPLE SERVICE FOR
A SIMPLE CAKE IS JUST THE
TICKET FOR THOSE WHO
LOVE THE ELEGANCE OF
MINIMALISM. THIS DELIGHTFUL
PRESENTATION IS PERFECT FOR
A BACKYARD PICNIC WEDDING.

OPPOSITE: THERE IS PLENTIFUL
DETAIL ON THIS ORNATE
WEDDING CAKE, AS THIS
CLOSE-UP REVEALS. THE
PIPED BASKETWEAVE, SWAGS
OF FLOWERS MEETING IN
RUFFLED BOWS, AND ACCENTS
OF PINK VARIEGATED FLOWERS
BLEND TOGETHER IN PERFECT
HARMONY.

Molded chocolate: Chocolate or white chocolate can be melted and reshaped in molds, cut into shapes, or spread into a thin layer and rolled into curls.

The techniques and effects used today to decorate cakes combine the arts of the sculptor, the painter, and the florist, with a pinch of the finest architectural embellishment. Your cake can be made to look like quilted fabric, a stack of gifts, or even the Eiffel Tower. Cake designers use patchwork colors, airbrushed patterns

(continued on page 40)

PAGE 38: FONDANT COVERING THE SIDES OF THIS CAKE HAS BEEN QUILTED FOR A HOMEY, COUNTRY EFFECT. A SPLASH OF COLOR ON THE TOP AND MIDDLE TIER REFLECT THE HUES CHOSEN FOR THE WEDDING.

PAGE 39: A LUXURIANT BURST OF WHITE ROSES SPILLS FROM THE TOP OF THIS FOUR-TIERED BEAUTY. THE DEEP GREEN LEAVES ADD A HINT OF CONTRAST TO A VERY TRADITIONAL WHITE CAKE.

RIGHT: TWO SIMPLE TIERS OF STRAWBERRY LAYER CAKE MAKE A DELICIOUS ENDING AT A SUMMER WEDDING. THIS OFF-CENTERED BEAUTY, FROSTED WITH WHITE CHOCOLATE ICING AND DECORATED WITH A SPRINKLING OF CHOCOLATE-DIPPED BERRIES NEEDS PRECIOUS LITTLE ORNA-MENTATION, AND IS PERFECT FOR A SMALL CROWD.

created with edible paints, gold leaf, and sheer French ribbons to embellish their creations. Silver and gold dragées and sugared "jewels" add sparkle, columns add height, and fresh flowers add just the right touch of romance.

And topping it all off is the cake topper! Although some couples opt for the unadorned elegance of an uncrowned cake, most brides and grooms want their wedding cake to have a special, finishing touch on the uppermost layer. The typical plastic bride and groom of yesteryear have been replaced with porcelain figures, bouquets of fresh flowers, herbs, bows, antique urns, or even kitschy collectibles. Be creative in your choices: add an antique birdcage, a china teacup overflowing with fresh lavender, or a framed photograph of you and your fiancé.

THOUGH IMITATION IS THE
SINCEREST FORM OF FLATTERY,
MANY MODERN BAKERS ADD
THEIR OWN STYLE WHEN
CREATING FLOWERS FOR
THEIR PASTRIES. THESE BOLD
DECORATIONS USE DEEP COLOR
AND STRONG SHAPES TO
ENLIVEN THE SMOOTH BASE.

OPPOSITE: POP CULTURE OBJECTS FROM DECADES PAST HAVE ACQUIRED COLLECTIBLE STATUS IN RECENT YEARS, WITH BRIDE-AND-GROOM CAKE DECORATIONS PROVING VERY POPULAR. THIS OUTSTANDING COLLECTION OF VINTAGE CAKE TOPPERS ILLUSTRATES SOME OF THE MANY VARIATIONS ON THE THEME.

LEFT: A CLASSIC RENDITION OF BARBIE AND KEN ADDS A TOUCH OF WHIMSY TO THE TOP OF A WEDDING CAKE. IN THE YEARS TO COME, THESE SWEET FIGURINES WILL HANG FROM THE HAPPY COUPLE'S CHRISTMAS TREE.

CHAPTER TWO

SETTING THE STAGE

PAGE 44: THIS SILVER TRAY
IS TOO DISTINGUISHED TO
COVER UP WITH EXTRAVAGANT
ORNAMENTATION, AND
NOTHING SHOULD DETRACT
FROM THE DETAILS OF THIS
DISTINCTIVE CAKE. THE TABLE IS
SET WITH A BEAUTIFUL CLOTH
THAT PICKS UP THE FLOWER
PATTERN AND COLOR USED
ON THE CAKE, AND A FEW
CHAMPAGNE GLASSES AND
CAKE PLATES ADD THE
FINISHING TOUCHES.

OPPOSITE: THIS LUXURIOUS
AND LIVELY SETTING CRADLES
THE CAKE IN COLOR, CREATING
A FLORAL FRAMEWORK THAT
EMPHASIZES THE GARDEN-
THEMED CAKE.

LEFT: THE PLACEMENT OF THE
CAKE TABLE IS AS IMPORTANT
AS THE WAY IT'S DECORATED.
THIS MAJESTIC CAKE BY ANA
PAZ HOLDS ITS OWN AMIDST
THE TOWERING COLUMNS
AND ARCHES OF THIS OUTDOOR
SETTING. A PATTERNED TABLE-
CLOTH DRAWS THE EYE TO
THE AREA, AND THE DARK
RING OF FOLIAGE PROVIDES
A CONTRASTING BASE FROM
WHICH THE WHITE CAKE
SOARS UPWARD.

*W*ith all the thought and effort that have gone into creating your wedding cake, you will probably agree that it looks too good to be hidden away in the kitchen until dinner has finished. A cake table is the perfect solution. Decorated to complement your cake and situated to grab the attention of everyone in the room, a beautifully executed cake table can be the highlight for your reception decor.

Keep the cake's stand in mind as you plan the table arrangement. Some cakes are placed on flat boards that will not be seen as part of the display, but others sit majestically on stands that add to the overall look of the culinary masterpiece.

YOUR CAKE CAN BE BROUGHT
OUT AT THE END OF THE
RECEPTION IF YOU DO NOT
HAVE THE ROOM TO DISPLAY
IT THROUGHOUT THE EVENT.
RESTING ON A STABLE BASE
ON A WHEELED CART OR
TABLE, THE CAKE AND ITS
ACCOUTREMENTS CAN BE
SET UP BEHIND THE SCENES,
READY TO MAKE THEIR
SENSATIONAL ARRIVAL AT
THE PROPER MOMENT.

The cake table must be in harmonious proportion to the size of your cake. For the sake of stability, the tabletop should be at least twelve to eighteen inches larger than the diameter of the cake stand, but bigger is not always better. A lone wedding cake on a sixty-inch table will look silly, unless the cake itself is enormous. If getting a smaller table isn't an option, carefully arrange the cake with other decorative items on the table, so that it is not lost on the big surface.

A BEAUTIFUL CAKE STAND AND
A SINGLE ROSE: UNDERSTATED
YET ELEGANT. THERE ARE
NO RULES WHEN IT COMES
TO DISPLAYING YOUR CAKE.
CHOOSE SOMETHING THAT
REALLY REFLECTS YOUR STYLE.

Regardless of size, select a beautiful covering for the table: perhaps a damask tablecloth, a layer of crisp dotted Swiss organdy over linen, or an heirloom quilt. Each of these suggestions would lend unique character to the table. Press leaves beneath a sheer cloth, or drape the sides with garlands of evergreen. Rose petals sprinkled randomly over the table's surface are simple yet striking embellishments.

THIS TOWERING TRIUMPH OF EDIBLE ARCHITECTURE MANAGES TO BE THE FOCAL POINT OF THIS ROOM WITHOUT OVERPOWERING IT. A CAKE OF SUCH PROPORTION AND DARING MIGHT OVERRUN A RESERVED DECORATIVE SCHEME, BUT THE DECOR AT THIS WEDDING INTRODUCES ENOUGH BOLD COLOR, CAREFULLY PLACED TO MOVE THE EYE AROUND THE ROOM. FLOATING TOPIARIES AND CANDELABRA CENTERPIECES REPEAT THE FLORAL MOTIFS OF THE CAKE, CREATING A UNIFIED AND WONDERFUL EFFECT.

CONSIDER THE ELEMENT OF LIGHT WHEN PLACING YOUR CAKE TABLE. A SPOTLIGHT CAN PROVIDE ILLUMINATION SO THAT YOUR SHOWPIECE GLOWS AGAINST THE BACKDROP OF AN OTHERWISE DARKENED AREA. HERE, THE ADDED VOTIVE CANDLES—CAREFULLY PLACED TO AVOID EXPOSURE DURING THE CAKE-CUTTING CEREMONY—TWINKLE LIKE THE LIGHTS SPARKLING IN THE NIGHT OUTSIDE.

Be sure to leave room on the table for the cake knife and cake server. These beautiful pieces may be part of a family legacy, given to you by your favorite aunt, or merely a beautiful utensil that you already own. Dress them up with a bouncy bow of organza or a lavish length of satin, attach a cluster of lilac tied with tulle, or fasten an herbal bouquet to the handle with long strands of raffia. When the time comes to cut and serve your cake, these cherished tools will be more than just decorations.

WHICH CAME FIRST: THE
UNDULATING CAKE STAND
RIMMED IN GOLD OR THE
GOLD-EDGED FONDANT
RIBBON CASCADING FROM
THE CAKE TOP? THE EFFECT
IS A TOTAL DELIGHT FROM TOP
TO BOTTOM, AND NEEDS NO
FURTHER ENRICHMENT.

As for the cutting of the cake, some choose to have the ceremony early in the

reception. The cake is whisked away, cut into slices behind the scenes, and served

at the end of the meal. Other couples opt to highlight the wedding cake through-

out the reception, building anticipation until the cake-cutting ceremony, which is

usually the last formal event of the evening. Don't underestimate the importance

of this ceremony. Some modern couples choose to omit certain traditional rituals,

(continued on page 56)

THE LAVENDER CLOTH
USED FOR THE TABLE SETTING
ENHANCES THE DEEPER PURPLE
SHADE OF THE GRAPE CLUSTERS
PIPED ONTO THIS JOYFUL
CONFECTION. VINES OF IVY
DRAPE THE CLOTH'S SURFACE
TO MIMIC THE IVY FROSTING
DRAPING THE CAKE, WHILE
THE FOOTED CELADON STAND
FORMS A BRIDGE BETWEEN
TABLE AND CAKE.

OPPOSITE: THE SEASIDE SETTING
FOR THIS WEDDING LENDS
ITSELF TO CASUAL DÉCOR,
AND THIS WEATHERED METAL
BEACH TABLE IS STYLISH
(AND STURDY!) *AU NATUREL*.
A SMATTERING OF SHELLS ON
THE TABLETOP ECHO THE EDIBLE
DECORATIONS ON THE CAKE.

LEFT: FRUIT IS A DAZZLING
ALTERNATIVE TO FLOWERS FOR
ADORNING BOTH CAKE AND
TABLE. FOR AN OUTDOOR
WEDDING, PLACE THE CAKE IN
A SHADED AREA TO KEEP IT AS
COOL AS POSSIBLE.

such as the bouquet toss or the newlyweds' introduction as Mr. and Mrs. The cutting of the cake is a charming collaborative gesture, however, and one that guests eagerly anticipate.

Consider how your cake will be served, and what it will look like after it has been sliced and plated. If you love ornate presentation of food, ask your caterer to dress each plate with a sprinkling of powdered sugar, a cluster of champagne grapes, or a beautiful royal icing flower to match those on your cake. Not your style? If you're a follower of the "less is more" theory, a fork may be all the accompaniment a piece of your delicious wedding cake needs.

OPPOSITE: ROMANCE IS IN BLOOM IN THIS MAGNIFICENT ALFRESCO SETTING. YARDS AND YARDS OF BILLOWING TULLE ARE GATHERED AROUND THE SIDES OF THE TABLE AND ALLOWED TO MEANDER GRACEFULLY ONTO THE FIELD BELOW. GARLANDS OF IVY BRING ALL EYES TOWARD THE CENTER OF THE TABLE, WHERE THE WEDDING CAKE DOES DOUBLE DUTY AS BOTH DESSERT AND CENTERPIECE.

LEFT: HAND-CROCHETED DOILIES DAINTILY PEEK OUT BENEATH A WREATH OF FRESH FLOWERS, IVY, AND SUGARED FRUITS, ALL OF WHICH ARE REPEATED ON THIS WEDDING CAKE'S TOP TIER. WITH EDIBLE SUGARED PANSIES PRESSED DIRECTLY INTO THE CAKE'S FROSTED SIDES, AND ITS GOLDEN SCROLLS AND RIBBON, THIS CONFECTION MANAGES TO LOOK BOTH MODERN AND ANTIQUE AT THE SAME TIME.

LEFT: CLUSTERS OF FRESH FLOWERS MOVE THE EYE ALL AROUND THIS BUTTERCREAM BEAUTY. A SIMPLE PIPED BORDER FINISHES THE EDGES. THIS TRADITIONAL CAKE NEEDS NOTHING MORE THAN A SMATTERING OF SIMILAR FLOWERS CIRCLING THE CAKE TABLE AND A FRAME OF TWO ARRANGEMENTS SET IN URNS ATOP MARBLE PILLARS TO POLISH ITS PRESENTATION.

OPPOSITE: HERE, AN UNEXPECTED SHOCK OF COLOR TRANSFORMS A VERY TRADITIONAL CAKE. CREATED BY MICHAEL MARTIN OF SAN FRANCISCO'S PERFECT ENDINGS, THIS RICHLY COLORED BEAUTY FEATURES HANDMADE DEEP PURPLE GRAPE CLUSTERS, WHILE DRAPED FONDANT "FABRIC" CONNECTS EACH TIER TO THE NEXT. WITH A SIMPLE SETTING—A WELL-PROPORTIONED TABLE COVERED WITH A CLASSIC WHITE CLOTH—THIS VERSATILE CAKE FITS EVERY LEVEL OF FORMALITY AND EVERY SEASON.

A SIMPLE BOARD ATOP A
LACE-COVERED TABLE IS
ALL THAT IS NEEDED FOR
SUPPORT, SO AS NOT TO
DRAW ATTENTION AWAY FROM
THE EXQUISITE FLOWER AND
RIBBON DECORATIONS THAT
ADORN THIS WEDDING CAKE.
THE LACE USED FOR THE
TABLECLOTH CAN MATCH THE
LACE ON THE BRIDE'S DRESS.

EDIBLE EMBELLISHMENT IS
ALWAYS AN OPTION. THIS
BLOOMING BASKETWEAVE
CAKE CAN BE SURROUNDED BY
OTHER DESSERT OPTIONS, SUCH
AS PETITS FOURS OR TRUFFLES.

OPPOSITE: FRESH ROSES PEEK
OUT BETWEEN EACH TIER
OF THIS LOFTY CREATION,
ASCENDING TO AN APEX OF
INTENSE BEAUTY. TO AVOID
DRAWING THE EYE AWAY FROM
THE FOCAL POINTS OF THE
CAKE, A SMATTERING OF ROSE
PETALS AND A FEW CAREFULLY
PLACED BLOOMS ARE ENOUGH
TO DECORATE THIS TABLETOP.

LEFT: A WEDDING IS THE
PERFECT OCCASION TO BREAK
OUT THE FAMILY SILVER. THE
ELEGANT SCROLLWORK AND
WHITE CHOCOLATE CURLS ON
THIS CAKE WITH OLD-WORLD
CHARM ARE ENHANCED BY THE
EXTRAVAGANT TABLE SETTING.
THIS MAGNIFICENT ANTIQUE
CAKE STAND ALSO HOLDS AN
HEIRLOOM CAKE KNIFE TIED
WITH A BOW.

RIGHT: THIS FESTIVE TABLE
BELONGS AT A PARTY! THE
EYE-CATCHING TABLE DRESSING,
ENCIRCLED WITH A BOUNTIFUL
FLORAL WREATH, ENHANCES
THE SIMPLE DECORATIONS ON
THE WEDDING CAKE.

OPPOSITE: IT'S HARD TO
TELL WHICH IS MORE BREATH-
TAKING, BUT THIS LAVISH
CAKE AND FESTOONED TABLE
PERFECTLY COMPLEMENT EACH
OTHER. THE ARCH LADEN WITH
FLOWERS AND FOLIAGE ATOP A
TABLE SKIRT AS FULL AS THE
BRIDAL GOWN FRAMES THE
DESSERT SHOWPIECE. THE
CAREFULLY-PLACED BOUQUET
OF FLOWERS ON THE FLOOR
ADDS AN EXTRA TOUCH THAT
COMPLETES THE PICTURE.

CHAPTER THREE

SWEET SURPRISES

PAGE 66: FOR YOUR FRIENDS
AND FAMILY WITH A SWEET
TOOTH, HERE'S THE PERFECT
GIFT . . . INDIVIDUAL SERVINGS
OF CAKE, ALL WRAPPED UP FOR
YOUR HOLIDAY WEDDING.

OPPOSITE: LITTLE CAKES CAN
MAKE A BIG IMPRESSION.
HERE, A TEMPTING PYRAMID
OF CHOCOLATE CUPCAKES
TOWERS OVER GUESTS AT
A RETRO-STYLED OUTDOOR
WEDDING. WHILE THE CUPCAKE
TOWER IS A POPULAR MODERN
INNOVATION, IT HARKENS BACK
TO THE EARLIEST WEDDING
CAKES, WHICH WERE ACTUALLY
PYRAMIDS OF SMALL CAKES OR
CREAM PUFFS.

LEFT: THIS HEARTY CAKE
CAN STAND UP TO A LOT OF
PATTERNING IN THE TABLE
SETTING AND SERVING PIECES.
WEDGES OF CHOCOLATE
GANACHE SEPARATE LAYERS
OF MOCHA CHIP CAKE.

*F*or those who believe dessert offers the best creative opportunities, there's a whole grab bag of alternative wedding cake ideas that can satisfy and surprise. Your wedding theme is a good starting point. A beach wedding might feature a cake covered with chocolate seashells and caramel "coral." A garden wedding cake could be made to look like a basket of freshly picked wildflowers attended by hovering butterflies. Are you using rainbow colors for the bridesmaids' dresses and table settings? Your cake might feature a cascade of rainbow-colored flowers falling from tier to tier, or a gum paste rainbow running from the base to the top layer, ending in a pot of gold on the uppermost tier.

Does your wedding date coincide with a holiday? Stacks of Victorian heart-shaped cakes frosted in pink or ivory and decorated with lace doilies made of royal icing are charming for Valentine's Day. Don't be afraid to use the red, white, and blue theme for your Independence Day wedding. Inspiration might also come from the season. For example, you may choose vibrant yellows, oranges, reds, and greens for a fall wedding, and decorate the cake table with pumpkins, gourds, and fallen leaves. The wedding cake can reflect the couple's ethnic culture, interests, hobbies, or personal style.

Even an ultra-formal affair can feature a non-traditional cake. Consider using your cake as your "something blue:" cutting-edge designers have made cakes that look like Wedgwood, Delftware, and wintry ice palaces. Wedding cake "gifts" are also very popular today. In this design, cake layers—stacked one upon the next—are covered in smooth fondant decorated to look like wrapped boxes, and each layer is adorned with an edible ribbon or bow. Yet another fun trend is to serve individual mini-wedding cakes—extraordinarily elegant miniatures of a two- or three-tiered wedding cake sized for a single portion.

And don't forget the groom's cake. This charming Southern tradition has migrated to all parts of the country and become quite a popular wedding trend. Groom's cakes come in all flavors and shapes, and generally reflect something personal about the groom himself. A love of fishing, for example, might translate into a sheet cake depicting a sea of fish biting everywhere except where the lone fisherman sits in his boat. On the other hand, a man with a serious sweet tooth might not care what the cake looks like, as long as it's chocolate, chocolate, and chocolate.

(continued on page 80)

OPPOSITE: BITE-SIZED TREATS ARE CREATED WITH LOVE FOR EVERYONE'S ENJOYMENT. THESE INDIVIDUAL "CAKES" ARE REALLY CHOCOLATE-DIPPED OREO COOKIES, SPRINKLED WITH NONPAREILS AND DECORATED WITH ROYAL ICING FIGURES.

OPPOSITE: IF THE WEDDING
CAKE EVOKES IMAGES OF THE
BRIDE IN HER WHITE DRESS,
THE GROOM IS CERTAINLY
ENTITLED TO THIS VERY
PERSONAL INTERPRETATION
OF THE GROOM'S CAKE. THE
EPITOME OF THE GENRE, THIS
TONGUE-IN-CHEEK CREATION
DESERVES ITS OWN PLACE OF
HONOR AT THE RECEPTION.

LEFT: A WEDDING CAKE CAN
BE ORNATE AND UNDERSTATED
AT THE SAME TIME, AS WITH
THIS STUNNING "GILDED LILY"
CAKE FROM PERFECT ENDINGS,
DECORATED WITH A CASCADE
OF HANDMADE, EDIBLE
CALLA LILIES.

OPPOSITE: YOUR CAKE DOESN'T HAVE TO LOOK LIKE A CAKE AT ALL! HERE, THE WEDDING CAKE MASQUERADES AS A STACKED SET OF BERIBBONED HAT BOXES.

LEFT: THIS HARLEQUIN-MOTIF CAKE WOULD BE EQUALLY AT HOME AT EITHER A SPRING OR WINTER WEDDING. THE SUBTLETY OF WHITE AND IVORY, IN CONTRAST WITH THE GREEN IVY AND WHIMSICAL PEA PODS, GIVES THE CAKE A STATELY POSTURE.

RIGHT: HERE, AN ECLECTIC
COMBINATION OF TECHNIQUES
IS USED TO PERFECTION.
REPETITION OF COLOR UNIFIES
THE TIERS, EVEN THOUGH THE
SURFACE EMBELLISHMENT ON
EACH LAYER IS DIFFERENT.

OPPOSITE: THE BOTTOM TIER
OF THIS CAKE HAS A MOST
UNUSUAL SHAPE, AND THE
POINTS AND CURVES ARE
REPEATED IN THE PATTERNS OF
THE FROSTING. AIRBRUSHING
EDIBLE TINTS ONTO THE
FROSTING ADDS DIMENSION
TO THE COLOR USED ON THIS
CAKE, WHICH IS ALL DECKED
OUT FOR A WINTER WEDDING.

OPPOSITE: EACH LAYER
OF THIS FAUX MARBLE
BUTTERCREAM CAKE HAS
BEEN PAINSTAKINGLY HAND–
PAINTED WITH EDIBLE COLOR
TO PRODUCE A STRIKING
AND UNUSUAL SHOWPIECE.
SINGULARLY UNIQUE, THE
WORK OF ART IS ADORNED
WITH FRESH FLOWERS AND
CURLY WILLOW BRANCHES,
REPEATING BOTH THE COLOR
AND THE NATURAL SHAPES OF
THE MARBLEIZED FINISH.

LEFT: GOOD THINGS
COME IN SMALL PACKAGES!
THE PROPORTION OF THIS
WINSOME CONFECTION
IS DECEPTIVE, UNTIL ONE
NOTICES THE BRIDE'S GLOVED
HAND HOLDING THE PEDESTAL
OF THIS DELIGHTFUL CAKE'S
STAND. THIS DIMINUTIVE
DARLING FROM CAKEWORK
IN SAN FRANCISCO FEATURES
A LACE DESIGN PRINTED ON
SHEETS OF WHITE CHOCOLATE
AND FESTOONED WITH
WHITE CHOCOLATE ROSES
AND RIBBONS.

SET ON A MIRRORED SURFACE
TO EMPHASIZE ITS HEIGHT, THE
SIX STACKED TIERS OF THIS
CAKE ARE EACH ADORNED
WITH AN EMBLEM. YOU MIGHT
DISPLAY A FAMILY CREST OR
ARCHITECTURAL ORNAMENT.

Traditionally, slices of the groom's cake were individually boxed, tied with a ribbon, and stacked on a table near the door for the guests to take home. Superstition states that each unmarried guest who sleeps with a sliver of the groom's cake under his or her pillow will dream of their future spouse.

Whatever your choice, remember that your wedding cake should be a reflection of you and your groom and of the style of your wedding. With a plethora of possibilities awaiting you, you will eventually settle on the perfect cake for your wedding. Enjoy every moment of the delicious search!

A SIMPLE SHEET CAKE, ALL
DRESSED UP IN WEDDING
FINERY, IS ENCHANTING FOR
A SMALL WEDDING.

RIGHT: LAYERS OF ROSES ADD AN ARCHITECTURAL ELEMENT BETWEEN THE LAYERS OF CAKE. THE USE OF TWO COLORS OF ROSES ADDS YET ANOTHER DIMENSION.

OPPOSITE: GRACEFULLY SLOPING TOWARD LOFTIER HEIGHTS, THIS LOVELY DESSERT FROM SAM GODFREY OF PERFECT ENDINGS IN SAN FRANCISCO FEATURES HANDMADE HYDRANGEA BLOSSOMS AND LEAVES ON A SLEEK FONDANT-COVERED HEXAGONAL CAKE. RATHER THAN CULMINATING IN A BOUQUET AS THE FOCAL POINT ON THE TOP TIER, THIS STUNNING TOWER WEARS A STRIKING BOUTONNIERE INSTEAD.

RIGHT: THIS PICNIC BASKET
CAKE OF BERRIES AND SUGARED
PANSIES, WITH ITS FLUID
HANDLE OF FLOWING VINES AND
BLOSSOMS, IS SO OUT-OF-THE-
ORDINARY THAT IT WILL BE
REMEMBERED BY YOU AND
YOUR GUESTS FOREVER.

OPPOSITE: FOR A BEACH
WEDDING, A SEASHELL CAKE
IS A PERFECT CHOICE. RATHER
THAN HOLDING UP THESE
SHELLS TO YOUR EAR TO HEAR
THE SEA, YOU'LL BE POPPING
THEM IN YOUR MOUTH.
BUT DON'T EXPECT TO TASTE
SEAWATER . . . THESE ARE ALL
PURE CHOCOLATE.

RIGHT: EACH STACKED TIER
OF THIS WEDDING CAKE GETS
A DIFFERENT DECORATIVE
TREATMENT. THE INSIDE CAN
BE DIFFERENT AS WELL . . .
MANY COUPLES ARE OPTING
FOR DIFFERENT FLAVORS OF
CAKE FOR EACH TIER.

OPPOSITE, TOP: THIS PETITE
PASTRY LOOKS LIKE STAINED
GLASS, COMPLETE WITH
"LEADED" BEADING, AND IS
JUST THE RIGHT SIZE FOR
AN INDIVIDUAL SERVING.

OPPOSITE, BOTTOM: HERE'S A
GLAMOROUS TWIST FOR YOUR
DAISY-THEMED WEDDING. THE
FROSTING DAISIES ARE PAINTED
WITH EDIBLE SILVER POWDER.
TINY AND CHARMING, THIS
CAKE IS PERFECTLY SIZED FOR
A SINGLE GUEST'S PLATE.

RIGHT: LOVELY FOR DECORATING PLACE SETTINGS, CAKE PLATES, OR AS TABLE DÉCOR, THESE HANDMADE COOKIES FEATURE THE COUPLE'S INITIALS.

OPPOSITE: TIERED BOUQUETS OF PLEASING PROPORTION, ALL CREATED BY THE BAKER'S ART, ARE STACKED ATOP EACH OTHER, CREATING A RIOTOUS BURST OF NATURE'S BEAUTY . . . ALL EDIBLE.

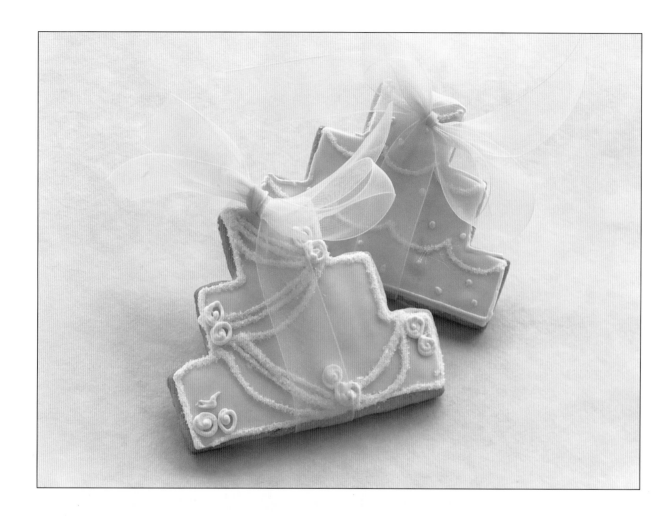

WHEN IS A WEDDING CAKE
NOT A WEDDING CAKE? WHEN
IT'S A COOKIE, OF COURSE!
CUT-OUT COOKIES CAN BE
DECORATED AS GAILY AS THE
CAKE ITSELF.

HEART-SHAPED SUGAR
COOKIES PIPED WITH THE
COUPLE'S MONOGRAM AND
TRIMMED WITH RIBBON ARE
A TASTEFUL—AND TASTY—
ACCOMPANIMENT TO EACH
SLICE OF PLATED CAKE.

OPPOSITE: THESE DELIGHTFUL HEART-SHAPED COOKIES, FROSTED WITH ROYAL ICING AND DECORATED WITH ELABORATE PIPING, ARE A NOTEWORTHY MEANS OF CARRYING YOUR "HEARTS-AND-FLOWERS" THEME TO THE DESSERT TABLE.

LEFT: ULTRA-FASHIONABLE, SMALL SUGAR BOXES ENCLOSE CANDIES, MINTS, OR NUTS, AND CAN BE USED AS FAVORS, PLACE SETTINGS, OR PART OF THE DESSERT.

Ana Paz Cakes
1460 NW 107th Avenue
Miami, FL 33172
tel: (305) 471-5850

Bijoux Deux Specialty Cakes
Contact: Ellen Baumwoll
304 Mulberry Street
New York, NY 10012
tel: (212) 266-0948

Cake Decorating by Toba
Contact: Toba Garrett
New York, NY
tel: (212) 234-3635

Cakework
Contact: Cecile Gady
613 York Street
San Francisco, CA 94110
tel: (415) 821-1333

Cheryl Kleinman Cakes
448 Atlantic Avenue
Brooklyn, NY 11217
tel: (718) 237-2271

Colette's Cakes
Contact: Colette Peters
681 Washington St.
New York, NY 10014
tel: (212) 366-6530

Gail Watson Custom Cakes
335 West 38th Street, #11
New York, NY 10018
tel: (212) 736-0705
www.gailwatsoncake.com

Margaret Braun
33 Bank Street, #17
New York, NY 10014
tel: (212) 929-1582

Perfect Endings
Contact: Sam Godfrey
San Francisco Bay Area,
tel: (510) 724-4365
Wine Country, tel: (707) 259-0500
www.perfectendings.com

Ron Ben-Israel Cakes
42 Greene St.
New York, NY 10013
tel: (212) 625-3369
www.weddingcakes.com

Sylvia Weinstock Cakes, Ltd.
273 Church Street
New York, NY 10013
tel: (212) 925-6698

You Take the Cake
Contact: Deborah Sigler
San Francisco Bay Area
tel: (510) 655-4651

Cakework: 78; ©Michael Bruk: 17; ©Peter Diggs: 2; ©Michelle Patte: 79

©Dennis Mock Photography: 33

©J. Duncan: 66, 81

©Tom Eckerle: 12, 18

©Elizabeth Whiting Associates: 62, 63, 64, 65

Envision: ©David Bishop: 13, 44; ©Steve Needham: 84

©Joshua Ets-Hokin: 23, 28

Food Pix: 32, 36, 41, 49, 61

FPG: ©Elizabeth Simpson: 82

©Michael Grand: 43, 69, 70, 74, 76, 77, 87 left, 87 right, 88, 90, 91, 92, 93

©Gregeiger Co. Utd, Inc.: 57

©Lyn Hughes: 10, 46

©Martin Jacobs: 16

Charmaine Jones: 85

©David Livingston: 42, 50, 55

©Bradley Olman: 27, 37

Ana Paz: ©Roy Llera: 3, 26, 31, 34, 35, 38, 39, 47, 52, 72, 80, 86

©Perfect Endings: 20, 58, 59, 68, 73, 83

Ron Ben-Israel Cakes: ©Simone Hele at St. Regis Hotel, NYC: 30; ©Guy Powers: 24, 25; ©Steve Skoll: 29

©Sarah Merians Photography: 48, 51

Stock Food: ©Eising: 22, 40; ©Greene: 60; ©Lieberman: 1, 53; ©Scherer: 6; ©Wondrasch: 56

©Dominique Vorillon: 54

©Gail Watson: 9, 15, 75, 89

A B O U T   T H E   A U T H O R

Bette Matthews is a writer and editor, and the author of *The Wedding Workbook*, a wedding planner also published by Friedman/Fairfax. Her writing focuses on cooking, crafts, and cats, which—along with coffee and chocolate—comprise what she calls "the C's of life." Bette's passion for cakes, particularly wedding cakes, falls into that category, and when she's not undertaking a new book, she works as a stylist with the New York caterer Eat Your Heart Out. Bette lives in New York City with her husband, photographer Antonio M. Rosario, and their three cats and pet mouse.